CW01638421

ISABELLA

by

GWEN FISHER SMITH

This book is dedicated to the memory of Isabella Chalmers

'Isabella'
is the first novel by
Gwen Fisher Smith.

Her second title 'Daisy's'
was printed in 2021

Cover design by Fiona Fraser

Praise for 'Daisy's'

This story, told through the eyes of a child, takes me right back to my own childhood and revives memories of a simpler age where children could safely be children, and enjoy freedom to roam in the Scottish countryside.

Mirren Jones, Author of 'Eight of Cups' and 'Never Do Harm'

Praise for 'Isabella'

A fascinating insight into the early life of a young Dundee girl Hardship, poverty and bereavement helped to form a feisty, hard-working and resourceful wife, mother and grandmother whose influence echoes through succeeding generations.

Mirren Jones, Author of 'Eight of Cups' and 'Never Do Harm'

ISBN 978-0-9560841-4-9

First published in Great Britain 2021

by EM People, Crathie Bridge,

Meigle, Blairgowrie, Perthshire, PH12 8QZ

ISABELLA

Isabella spends most of her time now nodding off in her chair as she sits with several other elderly women in the old folks' home she is now confined to. Isabella is now 98 years old and is unfortunately unable to walk.

She seems to be fairly cheery when we visit and we take her out as much as possible, but I suppose deep down she would rather be home in her own house, among all her familiar possessions. I think she must often sit and ponder over the old days when she had her sister for company and of course her husband, Norman.

She has told us many heartrending stories about her childhood and sometimes I wonder how she survived, but I do know for a fact she is a very strong-willed character and even at ninety-eight doesn't like anything to get the better of her. She has always been a very strong, rather domineering woman but then maybe she is like that because of all the knocks and upsetting times she has endured throughout her life.

Isabella's life began in a ground floor tenement block in Dundee's William Street. She had an older sister Robina and an older brother by the name of William.

Times were hard in those days – the year was nineteen hundred. Isabella and her Mother lived with her Gran, so there was very little room in the one bedroomed flat.

Her Mother worked in the mill as did many people at that time. She had no husband as her Mother (Isabella's Gran) did not like any of the men she had wished to marry therefore forbade any contact with them. Isabella was rather afraid of her Mother as she was very strict but she was very fond of her Granny.

Every morning before Isabella could go to school she had to dress her Granny and give her some breakfast, such a task for a little girl of about eight. Yes, times were hard but little did Isabella know what the next decade had in store for her.

Granny Isabella (centre) with from left: Mary Chalmers, Beanie Chalmers, Belle Chalmers, Eliza Chalmers, in front one of Belle's children on the left and Isabella on the right

CHAPTER ONE

'Isa dear, read the paper to me, meh eyesight isnae what it used tae be,' said Granny. Quickly she picked up the paper and read aloud so Granny would hear. 'Ye truly are a lovely reader and eh could hear every word affy clear,' she was told.

'Isabella, Isabella, ging and get some snuff for me and yer Granny then ging for a quarter gill at The Snug,' said her Mum. Isabella put out her hand for the money and her Mother warned her, 'Dinna you dare hae a play ootside first. Get the message and come back here or yer in for a hammerin.'

'Och, leave the bairn alane. She winna play first. Will ye Isa?'

'Oh no Granny, eh widna dare' said Isa, with a glint in her eye. Off she went along Alexander Street and met up with a couple of pals playing marbles in the middle of the road.

'Hi Isa. Want a game wi' us?' shouted the little girl.

'Just a quick game then,' Isa answered.

Isabella played with her friends for much longer than she intended and as darkness fell, she began to panic. She knew her Mother would be furious with her and now she was too afraid even to go home. She wandered along Alexander Street, gripping the money tightly that her Mother had given her for the snuff and whisky, pausing to look in some of the shop windows. Suddenly she heard a voice roaring at her.

'Hey, what are you up to wandering about here in the dark?'

Isabella spun round only to see a policeman striding towards her. She took to her heels and ran up a side street with the policeman desperately trying to keep up with her. He grabbed Isabella by the scruff of the neck and took her along to the Police Station.

'Now this is where you will end up if there's any more nonsense out of you,' she was warned. 'Right now, let's get you home.'

'Ma mither will batter me when eh get in,' Isabella told the policeman. 'Dinna let her hit me will ye no?' she asked him.

'Och come on now. She canna be that bad,' he said.

They reached the close and walked in towards the door. The policeman knocked heavily and Isabella stood behind him knowing full well what was about to happen. Her Mother answered the door.

'Mary Chalmers, I have yer lassie here. I found her wandering along Alexander Street.'

Before he could say another word, she grabbed Isabella, saying,

'You, ya wee bitch. Get in here 'till eh gie ye a hammerin.'

She slammed the door with such force that the windows rattled in the room. Isa was dragged by the hair into the kitchen and given a severe belting for not doing as she had been told. She was thumped on the back with a pair of bellows till her Granny shouted,

'Mary Chalmers, I'll get the bobbies tae ye for murdering that bairn!'

Mary Chalmers

She was sent to her bed with no supper and she had been determined not to cry in front of her Mother, but she did sob herself to sleep.

Isabella had a very close relationship with her sister Robina, whom she called 'Beanie' for short. Beanie called Isabella 'Bella' for short, so to most of their friends they were known as Beanie and Bella. Their brother's name was also shortened from William to just Wullie.

Although times were hard, the love between brother and sisters helped them through it. Going to school with no shoes was quite a common occurrence and people used to get by on bread and dripping, among other foodstuffs.

Every weekend, Bella's four uncles and three aunts would come to the house and all sit round and sing; they all had lovely voices. People would gather outside the window to listen to their fine voices. One of her uncles, Tam, had a five fingered belt which hung by the fireplace just in case he ever needed to use it on any of his sons, which he did, frequently! Uncle Tam had been blinded when he was working on the blasting for Balgay Cemetery.

Isabella's Mother took ill at the age of thirty-four and died of tuberculosis, such a heartache for a little girl who was not even nine years of age. After her Mother's funeral, Isabella and her brother and sister were sitting in their little flat when there was a knock at the door.

'Granny, there's somebody at the door,' Beanie shouted.

'Well, answer it then,' Granny said.

In walked a gentleman and a lady who introduced themselves.

'You're what? You're fae the Orphanage and ye think ye can just tak Isa awa?'

'Now, now Mrs Chalmers. Under the circumstances we think Isabella would be better coming with us.'

'Oh no Granny. Dinna let them tak me awa'. Eh want to stay with you,' Isabella sobbed.

'Dinna ye worry hen. Ye're staying richt here.'

'Now you twa bugger aff afore eh get the bobbies. Isa is no goin' onyplace. She's bidin' wi' me. So get!' Granny yelled.

They were shown the door very quickly and it was slammed behind them. Isa ran over to her Granny and flung her arms around her. 'Oh Granny, eh thought they were gonnae tak' me awa'. What a fleg eh got.'

'There is no takin' you onyplace lass. You're bidin' richt here,' Granny said.

CHAPTER TWO

Bella often thought about the times her brother would come home from the Army and meet their Mother at Gibbies' Mill. Sometimes her Mum would take her and Beanie to the station to meet Wullie coming off the train. She was so proud of him. Now that her Mother was dead, there would be no more meetings with Wullie at the Mill.

Time passed and every morning Bella was late for school as she had to see to her Granny. For some strange reason Granny didn't like Beanie so she would not let her help. It had to be Bella who did everything for her. Bella's teacher became so annoyed at her being late every morning that she started to give her the belt. Bella bit her lip every time the teacher's belt pounded her hand until eventually she had to tell Granny, who wrote a letter explaining to the teacher why Bella was always late. After that she was permitted to start school at nine thirty instead of nine o'clock.

One day when Bella came in from school, she heard voices in the parlour. There lying on the bed was one of her Mother's sisters, Auntie Annie.

'Bella, gie me that bottle fae ower there.' Auntie Annie pointed. Bella's Auntie looked quite distressed and was obviously upset about something. Bella handed over the bottle that looked like some kind of medicine.

'What's that yer takin' Auntie Annie?'

'What's in that bottle, Annie?' asked Granny.

'Och, it's no nothing fir you anes tae worry aboot,' said Annie.

She raised the bottle to her lips and drank; then she lay down and sobbed. Bella later found out that her Aunt had been upset about a male friend. After that her Aunt Annie died, which was that same evening. The doctor was called out and estimated the time of death to be around half past six. Death was due to poisoning.

Bella was questioned by the police. A statement was taken and some weeks later she had to appear at the Dundee District Court. Bella stood in the dock terrified and overawed by the whole situation. The prosecution were rather censorious but when all was said and done, the agreed outcome was that Bella's case was not one of malice aforethought.

Time passed on and things did not become much easier. Bella had to leave school at the age of thirteen to earn a wage. Her sister Beanie had now left home as she was six years older than Bella and of course Wullie was away in the Army. The sad thing about it all at this time was that Bella didn't even know where her sister was.

During the years after her Mother's death, Bella's brother had met and married a girl named Mary-Anne.

Wullie and Mary-Anne

Bella started a new job in one of Dundee's mills and before she reached the age of fourteen, her Granny died, leaving her completely alone and very upset. How had she managed to lose touch with her brother and sister, she would think to herself, puzzled? One of her Mother's sisters, Aunty Belle, came to take her to live with her and her family.

'Come on Bella. You'll hae tae come an' bide wi' us. No that we want ye, but we've nae choice!' Aunty Belle shouted at Bella.

Bella had to do exactly as Aunty told her as she was very afraid of her. She was a hard hearted woman and she and her husband became very violent when they drank too much.

Bella was dragged to Aunty Belle's house crying. Once inside, Bella realised just what kind of a life she was going to have, living with Aunty Belle, Uncle Micky and their two daughters, Annabelle and Minnie.

Bella nicknamed Uncle Micky, Micky Tricky.

'Get yersel' ower here ye wee pest!' Uncle Micky shouted to Bella. 'Now if yer bidin' in this hoose wi' us they ye'd better dae whit yer telt or I'll gie ye a hidin' ye'll never furgit, richt!' he yelled at her.

'Aye, Uncle Micky. Eh ken,' replied Bella.

'Upstairs Bella. Ye'll be sharin' a room wi' the lassies,' she was told.

She made her way to the bedroom and nearly died when she looked at the sheets on the bed.

'Eh cannae sleep on thae sheets. They look like they hivna been washed fur weeks,' Bella cried.

'You cheeky wee bitch. Dinna tell me eh hae a dirty hoose!' Aunty Belle screamed. She grabbed Bella by the hair and punched her so hard in the face that she blackened her eye. Poor Bella was just distraught and didn't know how she was ever going to be happy living there.

One evening, Aunty Belle and Micky Tricky were going out and told Bella she had to put Annabelle and Minnie's hair up in pleats.

'Dinna ye furgit Bella, get the lassies' hair up afore we get hame and I'd better no get ony excuses,' warned Aunty Belle.

Minnie sat obediently while Bella put up her hair.

'Right Annabelle, it's yer turn fur yer hair tae get done,' Bella said.

'Eh, that'll be richt. Yer no touching meh hair ye wee bitch,' shouted Annabelle.

'Look come on or yer ma will go scatty an' eh dinnae want intae trouble,' pleaded Bella.

'Awa' and loss yersel! What do ye think ye are onyhow? Yer no meh sister. We dinna even want ye here, do we no Minnie?' Annabelle shouted.

'Dinna be rotten Annabelle. Let Bella dae yer hair,' said Minnie.

After a while Bella gave up trying to persuade Annabelle to let her put up her hair.

Later that evening Bella heard her Aunt and Uncle come in the front door. They were fighting like two vicious cats. Aunty Belle came into the bedroom to see if Bella had done as instructed and the look on her face when she noticed that Annabelle's hair wasn't done was enough to make Bella shake in her shoes.

'Ma! Ma! Bella widnae dae meh hair. Eh asked her but she widnae,' yelled Annabelle.

'Ya bloody wee bitch that ye are! Eh telt ye tae pit up her hair, did eh no?' Aunty Belle screamed in her drunken voice.

'She widnae let me pit it up Aunty Belle. Honest, she widnae,' Bella tried to tell her.

'Bloody liar, em gonna batter ye fur this. Call meh lassie a liar wid ye?'

Aunty Belle got hold of Bella and battered her black and blue with a dustpan. She kicked and punched her till she couldn't get up. How Bella hated her life, being stuck with two people who obviously hated the sight of her. If only she could find her sister.

Auntie Belle, Isabella (centre back) and her three cousins

CHAPTER THREE

Isabella's life was just awful but she didn't know where else she could go. She couldn't tell anyone about the treatment she was getting from her Aunt and Uncle because she was too afraid. Annabelle was so horrid to her but at least little Minnie liked her. Sometimes Isabella would feed Minnie because the girl's Mother and Father would be lying drunk, unable to look after themselves, never mind the children.

'Hey you, bitch. Get doon tae the pub an' get us mair beer richt. There's the money and hurry up,' yelled Aunty Belle.

It was another drunken evening with two adults who were supposed to be responsible but were so drunk they could hardly walk.

Bella wandered along Alexander Street towards the pub to get the beer. Actually it was a trip she had made many times for her Mother and Granny but they didn't fight the way her Aunt and Uncle did.

Bella spotted a friend of hers coming along the road towards her. 'Hey Ina, do you ken whaur Beanie is? Eh dinna ken whaur she's moved tae an' eh miss her,' said Bella.

'Oh Bella, I've no' seen Beanie fur an age, so eh couldnae tell ye whaur she is,' she answered.

‘Oh God, I’m bidin’ wi meh Aunty Belle an’ eh hate her and her man. Eh cry him Micky Tricky. They’re aye batterin’ me fur nothing,’ Bella told Ina.

‘Eh ken them Bella. They are aye drunk an’ fight like mad, even in the street sometimes eh? Eh widna like tae be you havin’ tae bide wi’ they twa nutters,’ said Ina.

‘Och well, I’ll hae to go an’ get their beer. See ye later, Ina. Cheerio in the noo,’ Bella said.

‘Aye ok Bella. Tak care o’ yersel’ an’ hope ye find oot whaur Beanie is an’ get awa’ fae they crackpots yer bidin’ wi’,' answered Ina.

Bella arrived back at the house with the beer to find her Uncle drumming his fingers on the table. ‘Whaur in the hell hiv you been ya wee bitch?’ he yelled at her.

‘Affy sorry, eh didna mean tae be sae lang but an auld freend was gabbing tae me an’ eh couldna get awa,’ explained Bella.

Uncle Micky lunged at Bella and pummelled her body with his fists. With each blow Bella winced and screwed up her eyes, but not a tear rolled down her little white cheeks. She was a difficult case and not even Uncle Micky could break her spirit.

‘Hey Belle. You come ower her an’ gie her a thump an’ a,’ yelled Uncle Micky.

Aunty Belle walloped Bella so hard over the ear that she hurt her own hand.

'Why the hell should we hae tae look efter you?' ranted Aunty Belle. 'We didnae want you here but we've got nae choice. But we can easy get rid o' ye!' she screamed in Bella's ear.

When both her Aunt and Uncle were done physically abusing her, Bella made her way to the bedroom. Her body ached and her head pounded so hard she thought it would burst.

'Oh Beanie, where are you?' Bella sobbed.

She heard Annabelle and Minnie coming in the room.

'Oh dear. Look at poor wee Bella, she's been greetin,' laughed Annabelle.

'Dinnae be sae rotten tae her. She a'richt really,' said Minnie. 'Are you ok Bella? Did ye get an affy doin' fae ma Mum and Dad?' asked Minnie.

'Eh dinna want tae bide here. Eh just want tae find meh sister,' said Bella, trying not to cry in front of Annabelle. Bella hated Annabelle just about as much as she hated Aunty Belle. They were two of a kind - hard, uncaring, rough and cold hearted.

Bella dragged herself out of bed the next morning to go to work at the biscuit factory where she managed to get a job. The hours were long and hard from six in the morning till six at night, with only a short break for lunch in between. What a boring job it was, putting the icing on the biscuits. At least it was a job but it was poorly paid and Aunty Belle took most of her wages and spent the majority of it on drink.

The hooter for finishing time blasted out at six o'clock and Bella dragged herself out of the factory doors to begin her walk home. Suddenly she heard her name being shouted from across the street.

'Bella, Bella. Get yersel' ower here richt now. Em needin' money fae ye'.'

Bella cringed when she saw who was shouting. It was Aunty Belle.

'Eh dinna hae hardly ony money tae gie ye,' Bella told her.

'Just gee's what ye've got an' hurry up,' demanded her Aunt, holding out her hand just ready to grab what Bella could find in her pocket.

'Look, that's a' that there is, an' eh'm needing tae keep that fur masel' fur the rest o' the week till pey day,' Bella tried to explain to Aunty Belle.

'Ye selfish wee bloody bitch. An' tae think eh'm keepin' ye and ye'll no even gie me spare money. Ye're gonna get a hidin' fur that. Just ye wait and see, you bloody wee organ grinder!' yelled Aunty Belle.

Bella was grabbed by the arm and pulled along the road towards the dingy wee flat that was unfortunately her home. Aunty Belle pulled Bella in every closie entrance and thumped her as hard as she possibly could.

'See when eh get ye hame, eh'm gonna mak' sure ye dinna get nothin' fur yer tea an' ye can get doon tae the wash-hoose an' dae the washing an' a. An' ye can scrub till yer fingers are a' sare, ye bloody organ grinder!' yelled Aunty.

When they arrived back at the stinking hole Aunty Belle called home, Bella took all the washing down to the wash-house and started scrubbing. She had been down there for ages when she suddenly realised she couldn't do another thing; she was so tired. She leaned her arms on the sink, then her head, and sobbed quite uncontrollably.

The backies of the tenement building

CHAPTER FOUR

Bella had lived with her Aunty for almost a year and still could find no trace of her sister. She had been mentally abused by these relatives and beaten and thrown about. She just didn't know how much more she could take.

It was nearing the end of April 1915 and another winter nearly over, but the winds could still be cruel. She looked out of the window and watched as the clouds sped across the sky to some unknown destination.

Some days Bella could hardly utter a word for the lump in her throat as she thought of her sister Beanie. She prayed to God that one day, perhaps one day, she would find her.

One horrid evening after her Aunt and Uncle had come home drunk, there was a big fight in the scullery between the two of them.

'Dinna think yer sleeping in meh bed,' yelled Aunty Belle to Uncle Micky.

'Wha wants tae sleep wi' you onyhow ye auld bag,' answered her Uncle.

Annabelle and Minnie were sound asleep but Bella heard every word even though she tried to cover up her ears.

'Get the hell oot o' meh road an' git tae yer bed but dinna dare go in mines or see me, ye'll get a knife in yer back when yer sleepin'!' Aunty Belle screamed at the top of her voice.

Bella lay and listened to the door closing and could hear footsteps in the lobby which seemed to be making their way up towards the room she was in with the two girls. Slowly the door handle turned and Uncle Mikey stotted into the room. He was breathing heavily and muttering to himself about Aunty Belle being a bitch and an old bag, and for the first time in her life Bella agreed with him although she had to do so in her thoughts.

Bella wondered to herself where her Uncle was going to sleep as there was no other bed in the room apart from the one she and the girls shared.

Suddenly the covers were ever so gently pulled off Bella, and her Uncle slid beneath the sheets behind her. Bella lay in a complete state of fear, unable to move. The inevitable began to happen. Uncle Micky's hand ran over Bella's body but she was in no way going to allow this dirty drunken brute touch her sexually without putting up a fight. She jumped out of bed and screamed and screamed till she was hoarse. Uncle Micky grabbed his clothes and fled from the house.

Needless to say Aunty Belle was so drunk that even taking a brass band to her bedside would never have wakened her. Annabelle and Minnie wakened up and wondered what all the commotion was about but Bella didn't tell any of them.

Several days passed. Aunty Belle was so quiet because Uncle Micky had gone but she didn't know why or where until a telegram arrived. Uncle Micky was in Glasgow in a model lodging house and Aunty Belle was to join him with the children right away. They all had to help Aunty to get things organised but Bella was more heartbroken than ever now because if she was being taken to Glasgow then she would never have any hope of finding her sister.

As she and Aunty Belle walked along the Murraygate, they bumped into a woman called Margaret that Aunty knew.

'We're gaen awa' tae Glesgay tae bide. Micky went last week an noo we're gaen an' a,' Aunty told the women.

'Oh Belle, but yer no' takin' that lassie wi ye are ye?' the woman asked.

'She'll hae tae come, there's naebody else can tak her in so I've nae choice,' Aunty explained.

'Well, if ye dinna mind, I'll tak her, she can come an' bide wi' me.'

Margaret held out her hand to Bella and she grabbed it tightly. Bella for the first time in a long time felt happy and had an inner feeling that she would be very happy when she went to live with Margaret.

The Hilltown

CHAPTER FIVE

The following morning was rather overcast and a blustery wind was whirling fallen leaves along the pavements. Aunty Belle was not in the best of moods. She was heading off to Glasgow later that day with the two girls but at this moment was taking Bella to meet up with Margaret, the lady who offered to look after Bella.

'Will eh ever have to live with you again Aunty Belle?' enquired Bella.

'That will be richt. Yer no biding wi' me ever again, no if eh can help it,' answered Aunty.

Bella heaved a sigh of relief. The last thing she ever wanted was to see this horrible woman she was ashamed to call Aunty again.

In the distance Bella saw Margaret standing at the entrance to the Barrack Park.

'There she is standing at the park gate,' said Bella.

She raised her hand and waved to Margaret excitedly.

A strong gust of wind whipped Margaret's hat off and blew it right up into the air, and Bella chased after it, catching it just before it was blown over a garden wall.

'Here you are Margaret. Eh just caught it afore it blew richt ower the wa',' Bella giggled.

'Thanks Bella. Yer a good lassie, fir this is meh bestest hat,' said Margaret.

'Richt Margaret. Here's Bella fir ye. Noo eh'm gaen awa' hame tae get masel ready fir gaen tae Glesga. An' you Bella - ye better be guid fir that wumman cause if eh hear ony bad reports aboot ye, then eh wull cum hame an' batter ye,' said Aunty Belle.

'Don't ye worry aboot that lassie Belle. Eh ken she'll be nae bather tae me,' answered Margaret.

Aunty Belle turned and walked away and Bella didn't even say 'goodbye'. She was so happy to be rid of such a cruel, hard woman. She hoped she would never see her again for the rest of her life.

Margaret chatted to Bella as they both walked along the road towards her house. Margaret lived in a flat attached to a big house. She opened the door and Bella walked in.

'Oh what a bonny hoose, and a' thon bonny ornaments an' a piana an' a'!' said Bella.

'Come on lass an' see yer bedroom. It's affy bonny an' a',' said Margaret.

Bella opened the door that was to be her room for the time she was to spend there. It was a pretty little room, much nicer than the dump she had lived in with her Aunt.

'Eh hae a sister ye ken. An' eh hivna been able tae find her fir ages. But if she ever finds me, will ye let her bide here an' a'?' Bella asked.
'Oh well eh dinna really think eh wid hae the space, but she could come and see yer room if ye like,' answered Margaret.

'Now Bella. Eh understand yer Aunty widna hae been affy nice tae ye, but dinna worry cause ye'll be happy biding wi' me and ye'll no get hit or onything like that,' assured Margaret.

'Thanks affy much, Margaret. Ye ken it was affy biding wi Aunty cause she hated me sae much an' of coorse eh hated her an' a'. But dinna worry aboot me, cause eh winna bather onybody,' said Bella.

Margaret left Bella alone for a while to give her a chance to come to terms with her new surroundings. Bella fell into a deep sleep on the lovely clean single bed and didn't waken till late that same afternoon. She was a bit disorientated when she opened her eyes. Then she remembered where she was and was quite happy. The only person missing from her life was Beanie; if only she could find her.

Bella went out for a walk that afternoon to ask the folks around the Hilltown if anyone had seen Beanie. She suddenly saw before her the figure she remembered from a few years ago when her Mother had been alive. It was the policeman who had taken her home on a dark night. How she remembered the hammering she was given that evening.

Her memory travelled back to the days when her Mother was alive and she laughed as she thought to herself about her Granny of whom she had been very fond. There was many an argument in that household but there had been some good times.

Bella had been more fond of her Granny than she had been of her Mother. Her Mother had been far too strict and rather bad tempered where her Granny had been a bit more compassionate.

As she walked on along Alexander Street, she passed by the butcher's where the dark meat of cows and lambs hung, fly-ridden from meat hooks. There was a tobacconist's next door run by a little old man who looked like he had been there since the beginning of time.

'Hi there Bella. Whaur hiv ye been? Eh hivna seen ye fer an age,' came a voice from behind. Bella turned round to see an old school friend she hadn't clapped eyes on for quite some considerable time.

'In the name o' the wee man. If it isnae Wilamena Stewart. How are ye daen?' asked Bella.

'Och, eh'm no bad Bella. Whit aboot yersel'? Whaur are ye bidin'?' she asked.

Bella told her old school chum about Aunty Belle and she was gob-smacked at the thought of poor Bella having to stay with them.

‘Oh meh goad Bella. It must hae been bloody affy haen tae bide wi’ them. They are a richt bad lot. Bet yer glad yer awa’ fae them noo,’ said Wilamena.

They both stood and chatted for some time, catching up on all the news, then waved each other goodbye with Wilamena promising to get in touch if she saw Beanie

CHAPTER SIX

Hope was keeping Bella going after the many years of suffering and heartbreak; the hope of seeing her sister again one day.

Beanie

Bella lived happily with Margaret who really had been a godsend at a time in Bella's life when every waking minute had become a trauma and a nightmare. She hoped now that God was giving her a helping hand through part of her life. Margaret fed Bella quite well and allowed her to play the piano that stood behind the lounge door. Bella loved the sound of the piano. Though she was no expert, she loved to tinker about on it, with a little singing thrown in.

Bella did her share of the washing, pouring buckets of hot water into the tub and rubbing the clothes on the corrugated washboard. Though she kept busy between her work in the biscuit factory and her chores at home, it did not ease her feeling of emptiness; the severed contact with her sister was almost like a death. If only she could hear some news of Beanie.

One evening Bella sat by the window watching the clouds race through the sky to some unknown destination and pondered over her life. She hadn't had many happy times, although it hadn't all been bad. The most harrowing time had been the year or so spent with Aunty Belle.

Disturbing her thoughts, Margaret entered the room and they both sat and chatted about mundane things, leaving Bella feeling rather bored. Margaret was such a kind woman but could be ever so boring.

'Now Bella, when yer in the toon the morn, ging intae Cantrells an' get some fish fur the tea,' Margaret told Bella.

'Aye, ok. Eh'll ging in fae meh work, cause eh'm feenished at fower the morn,' Bella answered.

'Now mind an' get biggish butties o' fish; nae wee totty anes.'

Bella shook her head in agreement and Margaret left the room. Bella could hardly wait to get the fish the following day. She had come a long way from the usual tea-time meal of bread and treacle from Aunty Belle. Every night had been the same, bread and treacle, bread and treacle, bread and treacle. My god, how Bella detested it.

There was a war on and certain foods were difficult to come by but Margaret at least made a good effort to have reasonably good food, and one bonus was that she didn't touch alcohol, much to Bella's delight. She had seen so many incidents and heard so many arguments over the last fifteen years that were drink-related.

Her Mother and Granny would shout at each other when they had been drinking. Sometimes her Mother would fall asleep on the floor after an evening binge and no-one would dare try to move her. Bella once tried to move her Mother but learned very quickly not to try a second time. Then of course she saw with her Aunty and Uncle just the effect too much alcohol could have. They were wicked enough without it and ten times worse boozed up.

Bella did some knitting that evening for the soldiers. She was quite an expert at knitting socks and balaclavas for the army lads and she was sure without a doubt that they would be forever grateful to all the women who sent knitted garments for them. She could imagine them stuck in some muddy and damp trench, or lying in their beds hearing the constant sounds of gunfire.

Bella had not heard from her brother for a long time and sometimes wondered if he was alive or dead. She had rather a restless night and dragged herself out of bed the following morning, her head pounding like it would burst.

The rain was bouncing off the pavement as Bella made her way to work. Whipping winds curled round the branches of the trees and buffeted them about till they were almost bent double and touching the ground. Lightning forked across the sky and judging by the looks of the clouds, Bella agreed with herself that daylight was going to be very limited.

She worked hard that day and finished around four o'clock, then made her way to the fish shop as promised for the fish for Margaret. She walked through the town and up Constitution Road towards home. She could almost smell the fish frying in the pan; fish was her favourite and she could only thank God the day Margaret came along and saved her from a life of pure purgatory and an evening meal of bread and treacle.

CHAPTER SEVEN

Bella had now been lodging with Margaret for about three months. It was a Saturday morning and Bella was about to go to the swimming baths when there was a knock at the door. After a few moments, Margaret appeared in Bella's room.

'Bella, there seems tae be a lassie at the door fur ye,' Margaret said.

'But naebody kens aboot me bidin' here except Aunty Belle an' it'll no better be that auld bitch,' answered Bella.

She made her way cautiously to the front door and couldn't believe her eyes.

'Oh Beanie. It's you. Whaur hiv ye been a' this time?' cried Bella.

They both stood holding hands and Beanie cried 'Oh Bella, eh thocht eh'd never see ye again cause eh didna ken whaur ye were until eh met an auld freend o' yours last nicht,' Beanie explained.

'Eh ken whit ye mean but it's been affy fur me cause eh hid tae bide wi' Aunty Belle an' ye ken whit like she is. Honest Beanie, she was a dirty rotten bitch tae me an' so wis Micky Tricky. He tried tae dae an affy bad thing tae me but eh widna let him, Beanie.'

Bella's tongue went nineteen to the dozen telling her sister all about her traumatic time with her Aunt and Uncle.

Margaret invited Beanie into her house and made them both tea and scones; then she helped Bella pack up what little belongings she had.

'Well Bella. Eh will surely miss ye lass. It's been rare havin' ye here but eh ken ye'll be wanting tae gang wi' yer sister. So good luck an' mind tae keep in touch wi' me noo,' said Margaret.

'Thanks ever sae much fur a' that ye did fur me an' eh'll no' forget ye, dinna worry.'

Bella gave Margaret a quick hug and then she and Beanie made their way to Beanie's flat. She had a little and very basic flat in Jamaica Street. It was a low door.

'Come on Bella. We'll hae tae ging fur twa mattresses furst, fae a lassie eh ken. She wis gonna dump them; eh kent we wid need something tae sleep on,' Beanie laughed.

They hurriedly went along towards Nelson Street and reached the closie entrance.

'Here we are an' eh hope she no' oot fur eh couldnae be bathered comin' back efter,' Beanie said.

'Oh holy sufferin' Beanie. She'd better be in.'

Beanie rattled on the letterbox and eventually Muggie answered.

'Hey, hiya Beanie. Have ye come fur the mattress then?' asked Muggie.

'Eh Muggie, thanks. It'll be an affy good help. It's affy good o' ye,' Beanie answered.

Bella didn't say anything but she was also very grateful. It was good how friends would rally round to help in a desperate time of need. Bella had certainly endured many times like that. It had almost become a way of life; but she hated to ask anyone for anything.

Shortly after Bella moved in with Beanie, she managed to get a job beside her sister in Laing's Mill in Dura Street in Dundee. There was little banter in the mill, work was hard and often gruelling, but at least they had some money to put food on the tale and pay bills such as heating and rent. The hours were long, six till six, and the atmosphere hot and sweaty with all sorts of odours coming from so many bodies.

At lunch break one Monday, Beanie and Bella were having a bite to eat when an old friend of Bella's came towards them.

'Hey Bella, eh saw that auld bitch o' an aunt o' yours yesterday. Ken the ane ye were bidin' wi' efter yer Granny died?'

Bella almost choked on her tea.

'Ye saw wha? No Aunty Belle sharely?' stammered Bella.

'That's her name, aye. She was gaen doon Rosebank wi' a shawl wrapped aroond her shooders. A bloody proper mess she wis an' a'. Ye ken she even had a keeker,' laughed Bella's friend.

'Dinna tell us onymare. We dinna want tae ken,' Beanie said.

CHAPTER EIGHT

Bella and Beanie worked together well and were only too grateful to have each other back again. Eventually they found out where Wullie their brother lived and decided to pay him a visit. When they arrived on the doorstep, there was a very tearful reunion. There was so much news for them all to catch up on.

Bella and Beanie for the first time met their nephew William and three nieces by the names of Denise, Alice and Molly. There was such excitement and they were all so happy to be together again after so long. Mary-Anne, Wullie's wife, was a fine girl and Bella and Beanie seemed to get along well with her.

It wasn't long before Bella and Beanie were asked to go and live with Wullie and Mary-Anne. They lived in a low door in Lilybank, and although there would be very little room, it would be beneficial financially for Bella and Beanie, and also would be a help to Mary-Anne.

They moved all their belongings into Wullie's flat and they all lived just like one happy family.

Beanie continued to work in the mill but Bella was fed up with the hot sweaty tedious work and decided to go into service. She began work in a large house in Wormit. The first time she put on her uniform, she admired herself in the mirror. How she loved to be dressed so smartly with her crisp white apron with not a crease in it, and her little white hat.

She lived in, and was quite happy with her neat little attic room at the top of the house. All the usual chores had to be done like cleaning shoes and boots till they were gleaming and setting the lovely big table for mealtimes. Of course there was ironing and dusting, and of course announcing any visitors who called.

Bella was summoned to the study one morning to see the mistress.

'Isabella, please try to look at little more pleasant and make an effort to smile now and again. Honestly girl, your face is enough to turn the milk sour,' the mistress said to Bella.

'Yes Ma'am,' replied Bella.

Bella was absolutely furious at being told off. She wasn't of the nature of some people but was rather fiery tempered.

Time passed on and Bella remained in the big house working away with only one Saturday off in a month. She always took the Fifie into Dundee on those days to visit her family.

While cleaning the lounge one beautiful morning, Bella went over to the baby grand piano to have a closer look. It was so beautiful she could not resist sitting down and playing a tune. What was she doing? She knew only too well that if the Mistress were to hear of this, she would be in big trouble but she couldn't seem to stop her fingers flitting over the keys.

Suddenly she stopped as if she had abruptly come to her senses. She quickly closed the lid and carried on with her cleaning. After a short while the Mistress appeared and pointed to Bella.

'You girl, in the lounge, now,' ordered the Mistress.

The door was slammed shut.

'Yes ma'am. You want to speak with me,' said Bella so politely.

'Speak with you!' yelled the Mistress. 'Don't you ever dare touch that piano again. You know full well that you are under no circumstances permitted to tamper with anything in this house, and don't you dare forget it. Now get out.'

Bella left the room but she was so angry at being told off that the steam was almost puffing out of her ears. She handed in her notice and left her job.

'Now what?' she thought to herself as she made her way to catch the Fifie back to Dundee.

CHAPTER NINE

Bella was welcomed back into Wullie's house with open arms. The children were all very fond of her and had been saving up jelly jars so that they could go to the pictures. Oh yes! They knew good old Bella would take them.

Wullie and Mary-Anne (centre) with Beanie and Bella behind, two of their three girls in front

'Hey Bella. Whit happened that ye couldna' bide on in thon big hoose?' Beanie quizzed.

'Och Beanie. Ye ken me. Eh just couldna' keep meh hands aff the piana an' the Mistress aboot took a fut,' Bella told her. 'One thing led to anither an' eh just thocht tae masel' it wis time tae get oot.'

'Well Bella. We a' ken how ye live on a short fuse. Sharely the Mistress didna' ken,' laughed Beanie.

'Whit are ye gaen tae dae noo Bella for a joab? Will ye ging back tae the mill, cos ye'll get it nae bather?' asked Mary-Anne.

'It'll nae be ony bather tae Bella tae get a joab. She's a grand hard worker. As least that's whit eh was telt beh thon bloke wha used tae be yer gaffer,' Wullie piped up.

'Eh'll come doon the morn wi' you Beanie, an' see whit thon gaffer boy has to say aboot me startin' again,' said Bella.

Bella awoke the following morning her head spinning with all sorts of thoughts. What a terrible night's sleep she had had. No! She wouldn't go back to the mill. Bella wanted to do something different with her life even if it meant getting some kind of a different job.

'Hey Beanie. Eh dinna think the mill's such a guid idea efter a'. It's somethin' different eh want,' Bella informed her sister.

'Oh weel. Meh goad, mill no guid enough eh?' laughed Beanie.

'Och, it's no that Beanie. Eh'm wanting a cheenge fur eh'm fair seek o' the mill,' Bella tried to explain.

'Bella, eh'm only teasing ye. You dae whit ye want. It's bugger all tae dae wi' me but dinna come greetin' tae me if ye get a joab ye dinna like,' Beanie warned her.

Bella made her way down to the paper shop to get a daily paper and check out the Situations Vacant column to see if there were any jobs going. Plenty mill jobs were advertised and service jobs by the score. Aha! There was one for a company called Harley and Cox. Full time post for someone who wished to learn book-binding. Bella thought to herself – would she like to try that?

She went down into the town to Harley and Cox and was interviewed straight away and obviously made a decent enough impact on the manager for him to offer her the job there and then.

'Right now Isabella. You will be required to be here at nine o'clock on Monday morning and you will be expected to be punctual. I abhor lateness or slovenly work so you must understand these two things will not be tolerated,' she was advised by her new boss.
She was shown to the door and bade good-bye.

Bella made her way back to her brother's house, its walls visibly crumbled and stained, with windows that were lifeless. The frames were rotting and flaky.

Bella wondered if life would ever be much different or if there would always be a sameness about it. Her enthusiasm for more in life was easily dampened. She only had to look around.

She wasn't meant to be rich, but out there in the big bad world were many many people who were very much worse off than she. If she was in a selfish mood, she could easily become very angry at the way life had treated her so far, but little did she know then that life for her in the future was to be quite acceptable.

Although she would never be rich in money, she was to have quite a happy married life.

Jute mill workers

CHAPTER TEN

Bella could hardly wait to tell Beanie about her new job in Harley and Cox.

'Guess what Beanie? Eh've managed tae get a joab at the book bindin'. Wid ye believe that then?' Bella told her sister excitedly.

'Oh, so yer gaen tae gi' that a try are ye? An' how lang will that last eh wonder?' Beanie laughed.

'Och dinna bather aboot that. It's a cheenge fir me an eh canny wait tae try it but eh'll probably be hopeless,' Bella answered.

Bella settled in well in her new job although her lack of confidence didn't do her any favours. She had rather a volatile nature but in another sense she could be quite self-conscious and unco-operative, sometimes through shyness more than stubbornness.

The real stubbornness in her attitude became more prominent as she grew that bit older, as everyone was to see for themselves.

'Hey Beanie. Fancy gaen tae the sweemin' on Seterday? Eh'm getting a wee bitty fatter an' eh'll hae tae get rid o' it afore it gets ony worse,' said Bella.

'Aye, okay Bella. Whit time are ye wantin' tae ging? Aboot nine maybe? Is that early enough?' asked Beanie.

'Aye weel. Eh thocht aboot echt, mair like Beanie, cos it'll no be busy at a' at that time. It fair bugs me if a' they kids are mucking aboot an' splashin' a' ower the place,' said Bella.

'Och Bella, that means there's nae lang lie in then,' answered Beanie, tutting disgustedly.

'Richt. Dinna bather. Eh'll ging masel. Dinna bather aboot me, ya selfish devil,' was Bella's reply. Bella could really be so moody and quite cutting if things weren't going her way.

When Saturday came, they both did go to the swimming and did thirty lengths of the pool before any kids arrived on the scene. Bella and Beanie were both excellent swimmers, both rather muscly and powerful.

'Thon wis great, eh Beanie?' Bella said.

'Oh eh ken Bella. Eh feel great noo, just ready fur some ham an' eggs when we get back tae Wullie's hoose,' said Beanie.

CHAPTER ELEVEN

The year was now nineteen eighteen, and Dundee marked the end of the First World War with street parties and celebrations. Everyone was so happy to see the end of the hostilities and everybody spoke to everybody else; even people who had fallen out with each other previously embraced and cheered.

Bella was getting increasingly fed up with her job at the book binding and announced to Beanie that she needed a change.

'Eh micht o' kent,' Beanie laughed.

'Weel, nae wunder. It's affy boring ye ken Beanie,' Bella piped up.

'Look, eh telt ye tae come back tae the mill wi' me, but no, ye widnae dae it,' Beanie reminded Bella.

'Och eh ken Beanie. But I dinna want tae ging back tae the mill. There must be something else eh could dae, sharely tae god,' was Bella's reply.

'In the name o' the wee man Bella. Can ye no' just settle doon in the mill wi' me?' said Beanie. Beanie was beginning to get a bit rattled.

Bella started job hunting again and found a post at the baths in Nelson Street. Now that was a job to remember. People of all types coming in to have a bath; some clean enough but there was always an element of grubby, dirty, louse-ridden individuals who often left several of their bugs behind when they left the baths. How Bella could stand the job was a mystery to Beanie.

'Bella, get yersel' oot o' that feechie joab and get something else fur the love o' god,' Beanie told her.

'Ach eh ken it's no' the best joab in the world but eh could stand it for a whiley yet Beanie,' said Bella.

One evening as Beanie and Bella were sitting listening to the radio, Wullie came into the room with some news for Bella.

'Bella. Ye'll never guess wha' eh just met in the Snug; yer auld man Robert Dick. An' he's wanting tae see ye so eh telt him eh'd ask ye.'

'Whit the hell's he wantin'? He never bathered wi' me afore noo,' Bella shouted.

'Hey Bella. Maybe he's got a guilty conscience, eh?' Beanie laughed.

'Guilty conscience? Ye hae tae be kiddin' me noo, Beanie,' said Bella.

'Come on Bella. Jist meet him fir a wee while. He's no a bad bloke. Ye ken he's a' richt an' he really wants tae see ye,' said Wullie, in an almost pleading tone.

Wullie waited and looked at Bella for an answer. He could see she was very confused and very undecided.

'Okay then tell him eh will see him, but no fur lang,' Bella said.

Wullie was to organise a time and a place for them to meet and Bella had no intentions of going on her own. She wanted Wullie there with her. It was the first time she was to set eyes on her father and she realised it was going to be quite an awkward situation. The man might be her father but he would be a complete stranger.

'Richt Bella. Let's get on oor way tae meet your faither then,' said Wullie.

It was Friday night and Bella had been dreading this time coming but I suppose in a funny sort of way she was also quite curious. Would the meeting go well?

She and her brother walked to the top of Lilybank Raod and made their way to Nelson Street. All the time Bella's stomach turned over and over.

'Oh I don't know that I want to gae through with this,' Bella told Wullie.

'Dinna worry yersel' Bella. If ye dinna like him then ye need never see him again, ye ken.'

'Eh ken that, but whit dae eh cry him?' she said.

'Well ye could cry him Sir,' Wullie chuckled.

'Whit? Cry him Sir? Ye must be kiddin'. Eh ken whit eh'd like tae cry him though.'

Wullie had a habit of teasing Bella and this he did all the way to the front door of Robert Dick's house, just to try to stop her worrying. Wullie chapped on the door and they both waited with bated breath till it was slowly opened by a rather distinguished looking gentleman with rather a large moustache, curled up at the sides.

He stood and looked at Bella as if trying to almost study her face and probe into her mind. He needed to know so much about her yet didn't know how to say it in words. This lovely girl was his little lass of which he knew very little. What a waste. What a terrible waste.

'Come awa' in. It's affy nice tae meet ye,' he said, holding out his hand to Bella.

She glowered and certainly didn't offer her hand to him. He looked awkwardly at Wullie, looking for reassurance. Wullie shrugged his shoulders and gave him a look as if to say, 'Don't look for help here, matey. She's a real handful.'

'Well noo Bella. Let me tak a look at ye lass. Ye dinna really mind me o' yer mither, so eh think ye must tak thae good looks fae yer father.'

He laughed out loudly but Bella just stood and glowered at him.

They were led into a little front room, fairly tastefully decorated or at least as best as money would allow. There by the window sat a blonde-haired woman with her back to them. Bella couldn't see her face but did wonder who she was.

'This is my wife Jean,' said Bella's father. 'Jean, this is my daughter Isabella and her brother Wullie.'

There was total silence and it was so obvious that Jean had no intention of acknowledging Bella or Wullie. The atmosphere you could have cut with a knife. Bella's father tried to ignore the situation and carried on talking about the weather, and tried to find out as much possible about Bella but he was wasting his time. He could see that.

Bella sat with her head down feeling very uncomfortable, and poor Wullie was trying desperately to lighten the situation with chit-chat and jokes.

'Hey Bella, whit's tae dae? Cat got yer tongue or something?' asked her father.

'Dinna ken why ye want tae ken aboot me noo efter a' these years,' she answered.

'Yer meh lassie, and of coorse eh want tae ken aboot ye. It was circumstances that I couldna' help that kept me awa' fae ye.'

'Oh aye an' eh believe that an' a'. An' eh don't think,' said Bella. 'Eh'm gaen hame noo Wullie, so come on,' she ordered.

Wullie raised his eyes to the ceiling and replied, 'Right Bella. Anything ye say Bella.'

The lady at the window didn't turn round. Bella knew where she wasn't wanted.

Robert Dick showed them to the door and his parting words were of the guilt he felt not being part of Bella's life for all these years. But she didn't feel sorry for him, and neither did she believe him. He promised to visit her sometime but really she didn't care much either way.

She was quite a tough cookie and she was determined no-one would ever break her spirit even although she had been to hell and back many times in her eighteen years of life. She could cope with Robert Dick easily, because after all he was a stranger and he couldn't hurt her if she kept him out of her life – and that is exactly what she intended to do.

Robert Dick

CHAPTER TWELVE

On her way to work one morning, a rather kindly-looking gentleman doffed his cap to Bella and bade her good morning. Bella had seen him before but struggled with her memory to remember where she knew him from. Maybe it was Beanie's new husband Alec who had introduced them. Yes that was it. He was a friend of Alec's. It wasn't long after that when the gentleman in question stopped Bella on her way to work to have a chat and to ask her to go to the pictures with him.

'Oh well, aye. Eh suppose that wid be a' richt. Thanks very much,' accepted Bella, and they made arrangements to meet.

Before long they were inseparable. He was a lovely man, very kind, and of course he gave Bella her own way much of the time as it was easier that way. It didn't take Norman long to find out how difficult and stubborn she could be but most important of all, he loved her dearly.

Bella and Norman

They were married five years later in Dundee in the F and K Halls. It was a smallish affair but a lovely day for all. They had managed to find a flat in Dundee's Court Street and settled down to married life.

Norman and Bella with best man John Chalmers and Matron of Honour Beanie Carnegie

'Hey Bella, this is a smashing wee hoose here eh,' said Beanie.

'Aye, it's no' bad at a' Beanie. We should be here for a whilie,' said Bella.

'Bella eh've come tae tell ye Wullie and Mary-Anne are going awa' tae bide in Canada wi' the bairns, and Mary-Anne's mither is goin' an' a',' Beanie blurted out.

'Whit? Canada? But they cannae. It's too far. We wid never see them again Beanie.' Bella's voice quivered.

Wullie and Mary-Anne were packing up the house in preparation for the sailing to Canada which would take weeks. Packing things didn't take long as Bella and Beanie were both there to help.

'Oh Wullie. I wish ye wirna gaen sae far awa'. Will we ever see ye again?' Bella hugged her brother.

'Come on noo Bella. Do ye really want tae see a grown man greet?' Wullie tried to laugh.

'Eh really dinna ken Bella if we wid ever hae the money tae come back tae Dundee. But let's no talk like this. It winna be goodbye. It'll be cheerio an' see ye soon.'

Wullie gave Bella a playful dunt under the chin. It brought back memories of when he used to teach her to box. They had such fun as sparring partners.

Bella was never to forget the day Wullie, Mary-Anne and the children left on their travels for a better life in Canada. They all hugged and cried, and Bella pulled up little Wullie's socks for the very last time. She clung on to her brother sobbing because deep down she knew in her heart that it would be the last time she would see or touch him for the rest of her life.

Once they had gone, Bella and Beanie walked up the Hilltown to Stirling Street to visit Luke, who was Mary-Anne's father. Her mother had gone to Canada with them but her father had been left behind, for a number of reasons that are maybe better left unsaid.

As Bella and Beanie neared the door they could smell something cooking. Bella chapped on the rather grubby-looking door.

'Oh Bella, come on in. Hiya Beanie how're ye doin' then?' he asked.

'Well as ye can see, we wis greetin' a' the way up the Hilltoon,' Bella said.

'Look at me eh! Left sittin' here wi' a pan o' sassages, an' them awa' tae Canada. Bloody no real,' grunted Luke.

Bella and Beanie both helped Luke as much as they could until he died just a few months after the family had gone to Canada.

Arriving in a new land

CHAPTER THIRTEEN

Life carried on as usual and Bella wrote frequently to her brother whom she missed terribly. She was back working in the mill with Beanie. Norman was an engineer. Beanie's husband Alec also worked in the mill.

Now and again they would get a letter from Wullie telling them all about Canada and how different life was there. Bella liked to daydream and imagine herself going off to visit her brother but unfortunately the day didn't come until she was in her seventies, nearing eighty, and by that time her brother was dead.

Over the years Bella and Norman added to their family and had one son and one daughter, four grandchildren, six great-grandchildren, and one great-great-grandchild.

Unfortunately Norman was never to see any of his great-grandchildren or great-great-grandchild as he died in ninety hundred and sixty. Bella was heartbroken without him but her children were a great comfort to her. Her sister Beanie and brother-in-law Alec died within the following four years.

She often sits now and talks about 'The Old Days' and chuckles about the fun times they had. Every minute seems like an hour now as she sits in her chair in the old folks' home. She knows she will die there and at ninety-eight feels in a way that still being alive and unable to walk is like a punishment, but then how do any of us know where our lives will end. I will leave you with that thought.

Printed in Great Britain
by Amazon

62207952R00040